Polar Bear Pirates

and their quest to reach Fat City...

Not suitable for Bloaters

www.booksattransworld.co.uk

ABOUT THE AUTHOR

Milkman, policeman and salesman were just a few of the
many entries on Adrian Webster's CV before he moved into
the IT industry and discovered an extraordinary ability to
motivate and inspire others to achieve success. The son of a
Yorkshire coal miner, he has quickly established himself as
one of the most radical and entertaining motivational
speakers in the UK today.

Adrian Webster

Polar Bear Pirates

and their quest to reach Fat City...

A Grown-Up's Book For Kids At Work

Illustrations by Phil Williams · Polar Bear Pirate by Larry Rostant

BANTAM BOOKS
LONDON · NEW YORK · TORONTO · SYDNEY · AUCKLAND

POLAR BEAR PIRATES
A BANTAM BOOK: 0 553 81595 4

Originally published in Great Britain by Capstone Publishing Limited

PRINTING HISTORY
Capstone edition published 2002
Bantam edition published 2003

5 7 9 10 8 6 4

Copyright © text and illustrations Adrian Webster 2002, 2003
Illustrations by Phil Williams. Polar Bear Pirate by Larry Rostant

Set in Cartier Book by Julia Lloyd

Bantam Books are published by Transworld Publishers,
61–63 Uxbridge Road, London W5 5SA,
a division of The Random House Group Ltd,
in Australia by Random House Australia (Pty) Ltd,
20 Alfred Street, Milsons Point, Sydney, NSW 2061, Australia,
in New Zealand by Random House New Zealand Ltd,
18 Poland Road, Glenfield, Auckland 10, New Zealand
and in South Africa by Random House (Pty) Ltd,
Endulini, 5a Jubilee Road, Parktown 2193, South Africa.

Printed and bound in Great Britain by
Cox & Wyman Ltd, Reading, Berkshire.

Papers used by Transworld Publishers are natural, recyclable products made from wood grown in
sustainable forests. The manufacturing processes conform to the environmental regulations of
the country of origin.

This book is dedicated to all those who
believe in life before death.

For Mum and Dad,
Annie and Jack.

With special thanks to my wife Louise for being
my travelling companion and to
Seb, Harry and Rosie for keeping me on
the road to Fat City.

In memory of Paul Johnson.

Contents Page

Fat City

Fat City is where the winners live. Most people who live there came from Rock Bottom. No one has ever moved there from Complacency; that's where the Norms live, and to get there you go half way up the hill and turn off. The Nobodies all live in Quitter. It's easy to reach: you just stop.

There is a very small group of people who just won't give up trying to reach Fat City. The Norms and the Nobodies call them the Fools, perhaps not realizing that one day they'll be the ones to discover the hardest of all places to find: a place called Dignity where the Fools are all Kings.

www.polarbearpirates.com

Before we set off

Your Fat City

Fat City is wherever you want it to be, it's whatever you regard true success as being. Unfortunately very few people ever get to see their Fat City, so if you know where yours is and want to have any real chance of reaching it one day then you must start by asking yourself a few simple questions.

Have you got an egg in your fridge?

A lot of people would like to achieve a lot of things. They may have all the right experience, knowledge and more relevant degrees than a thermometer but they'll never reach their Fat City simply because they only want to and don't really need to. You can want an omelette as much as you like and have all the ingredients in the world in your fridge but unless you've got an egg it's probably best that you start thinking more along the lines of cheese on toast.

If you have an idea about what you want in life, the first question you must ask yourself is:

'Do I really have a burning need deep down inside to go and get it?'

It's extremely important that you think carefully about this and are deeply honest with your answer, otherwise you will just waste your most precious commodity – your time.

So many people spend their lives convincing themselves and pretending to others that they really are aching to make

it. Believing it to be their destiny, they go around boring the paint off walls and sending friends into deep comas with stories of how one day they're going to go out and hit the big time. Then when an opportunity comes along for them to actually do something about it they suddenly dig up more excuses than a delayed-train announcer. Worst of all, when they've missed the boat they go back to the same friends who have only just regained semi-consciousness and render them unconscious all over again, this time with their regrets of not having gone for it.

Whatever answer you give to the above question, it is in your own interest that you either go for it or forget it. Please, for the sake of your family and friends, don't let yourself get to the stage where nobody's in whenever you pop round.

Comfy cocoon for sale?

If you do have a true need to make it to Fat City, the second question you must ask yourself is 'Am I prepared to move, change and keep on moving?'

You can't expect everything to come to you magically while you stand still. If you want to improve, grow and live in Fat City you'll have to kick off your slippers and get a 'For Sale' sign up outside your comfy cocoon. Maybe you want to change but can't be bothered with all the hassle that's involved, or maybe you're worried about stepping beyond the confines of the cosy existence that you have come to know so well.

The choice is simple and very much down to you; you can

either stay where you are or you can move. You may be very happy where you are or, like a lot of talented people, you may at times feel like a truffle in a sewer, drifting along unnoticed and bogged down by mediocrity.

Moving out of your centrally heated cocoon and getting going is not going to be easy. Breaking old habits is at times going to be unbelievably hard and you must be prepared for things to get far worse along the way before they start to get better. Eventually when you do arrive in your Fat City, you will have to continue to change, to innovate and grow just to afford the rent. Stop developing and evolving and you'll be moving back in with the Norms.

If you should be in need of a little bump start, it may help you to know that Mother Nature ensures continued survival through ongoing transformation, sometimes sudden and dramatic and at other times subtle and unnoticed. The tiniest and most basic of creatures undergoes the most amazing metamorphosis to survive and thrive. As we all know, caterpillars turn into butterflies and tadpoles develop into frogs. When it comes to metamorphism these popular creatures tend to steal the limelight because of their acceptable, affable images, but even the lowest of the low can and do change. Some credit should be given here, I feel, to what in most people's minds is a specimen of pure disgust, a life form with a status ranking lower than the IQ of a clothes peg, the humble maggot. Yes, even these delightful little pods of displeasure see the necessity for change, sprouting their wings and buzzing off out of it!

Already got the Fat City T-shirt?

For those of you who regard yourselves as already having made it, and think you have found the formula for guaranteed ongoing achievement, I would like to take this opportunity to congratulate you and wish you continued success. At the same time, and without wishing to be like salmonella at a barbecue, I feel it only right and fair to offer you a few simple words of well-meant caution – 'complacency is the cancer of success'.

A self-licker?

You will find your chances of ever seeing Fat City are greatly increased if you leave your ego behind and you'll certainly get there a lot faster if you don't take yourself too seriously. If you are, by any chance, having a solo love affair and worshipping at your own shrine, then I'm sorry to have to burst your bubble with a few home truths. The simple fact is, that along with the rest of us, you are pretty much irrelevant in the grander scale of things, with probably far less than point one per cent of the population even knowing or caring that you exist.

If, however, you do think the whole world spins around you and that when you croak it will grind to a sudden halt for the rest of us, try signing your own name as big and as deep as you possibly can in the wet sands of a beach. Go mad, borrow a bucket and spade if you want to, then go back the next day and find your mark.

How many times when you've pulled a 'sicky' have you been genuinely able to enjoy your day off? The problem is that you can't really relax because you spend the whole day worrying that everybody at work is talking about you skiving. You feel so guilty that you convince yourself that you really do have the symptoms of the illness that you've told everyone you've got. Then when you go back to work the next day it's as though hardly anyone has even noticed that you've been away!

> ## Wake up! You don't matter, so lighten up, the pressure's off. What have you got to lose?

Sand writers

There are of course exceptions. Every now and then someone comes along who does make a difference; they make a real and lasting impact, they affect the world around them and leave behind their own unique imprint. What sets these rare people apart is their overwhelming and infectious love of life and their refreshingly simple approach to success. As firm believers in life before death they know how to play the game and reach Fat City. They are the Polar Bear Pirates.

The Game

Coming out to play?

The key to the success of these fun-loving but highly focused individuals is that as Polar Bear Pirates they regard their journey to Fat City as just a game, a fun race with winners and losers, a game based on attitude that anyone can play.

If you want to be a player it will involve you having to recognise and fight off some pretty ruthless and often highly elusive enemies along the way. It will require you needing to become a SONAR communicator – don't worry, you'll find out how – and if you are to have a snowball's chance of making it, you will have to familiarize yourself with and use a wide range of weapons, some of which you may not have encountered before. At times you will have to be incredibly devious just to survive. In addition, you must be able to stay focused on the game in hand whilst being exposed to a wide selection of career-warping viruses and, most importantly, you will have to rediscover a young child that you may or may not have seen for a while. Are you up for it?

Signpost Questions

To help guide yourself along the way you may find it useful to answer a number of questions indicated by Fat City signposts. Obviously the more honest you are with your answers the more of a help these questions will be.

The Polar Bear Pirate Information Desk

You may also find it extremely helpful to visit the Polar Bear Pirate Information Desk to obtain, exchange and share invaluable information and ideas with other Fat City travellers. As part of ongoing Polar Bear Pirate intelligence gathering you will be asked on occasions throughout this book for your highly valued and much appreciated input. Any questions or requests that require you to visit this interactive information desk will be clearly marked by the Polar Bear Pirate World sign.

To visit the Polar Bear Pirate Information Desk please go to **www.polarbearpirates.com**

Your 44.4

If you are ready to play, let's make a start by getting one thing into perspective. That is just how precious your time is.

Planet Earth is widely believed to be approximately 4,600 million years old. This is an unimaginable timescale, so for the sake of sanity, let's pretend that Earth is only 46 years of age. This being the case, mankind arrived here just four hours ago, JFK was shot about 17 seconds ago, Elvis died within the last 12 seconds and if you live to be a hundred you will only get 44.4 seconds. What you do with your go is of course entirely up to you but please remember life is not a department store, there are no refunds and the only two guarantees you get are that at some stage your clock will stop and that you will be taxed along the way.

How many seconds have you got left on your clock?

Your Enemies
en Route

The more success you have as a
player, the more of a target you will find
yourself becoming to a wide variety of
enemies along the way. Here are the most
commonly known ones that you are most
likely to encounter, to date. You may
well recognize some of them.

Don't feed the Neg Ferrets

Today's world is full of Neg Ferrets with insatiable appetites for other people's problems. From the moment they appear on this planet these intrepid warriors of doom seem determined to spend the whole of their 44.4 dedicated to seeking out and highlighting the negative side of life, as they machete their way through all things positive.

Drawn by some mysterious gravitational pull towards the downside, Neg Ferrets thrive on the misfortunes of others. When Apollo 13 took off hardly anyone was watching until five magic words were uttered: 'Houston, we have a problem.' Not content with their daily dose of negativity, fed to them through the media and a buffet selection of 'Worlds Worst' and 'From Hell' programmes dished up and repeated over and over again by chewing-gum television, some of them have developed into a new, advanced form of Neg Ferret, the Heat-Seeking Neg Ferret. This elite and ferociously ravenous species of whingers even set off on holidays armed with camcorders in the hope of filming such wonderful things as blocked drains and cockroaches. The best advice I can offer anyone when it comes to Neg Ferrets is don't go around moaning. The slightest of bleating noises will only attract them and gift them with an open invitation to feast, along with a few of their friends, on your problems.

At work these people are like little indoor clouds, always hovering around, drizzling doom and gloom on everyone.

'It'll never work... I'll give them three months... we've tried it before... this place isn't what it used to be... wasting our time... it's all going downhill... what's the point... I don't want to moan, but... we'll never make it... I'll bet it's rubbish... life's boring... we won't find a space... I hate Christmas... can't stand snow... it turns to slush you know...'

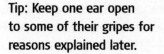

Tip: Keep one ear open to some of their gripes for reasons explained later.

Watch out for Sinkers

Sinkers are the disciples of your pear shape. They are those who have had little or no success themselves and have become obsessed with making sure that no one else has any either. Wanting everyone in the same below-average boat as themselves, they derive enormous satisfaction from using their sinking thinking to torpedo anyone attempting to reach Fat City. The chances of a Sinker being pleased to hear of your success are less than that of a vampire booking a beach holiday. Look out, the moment word of your success gets round there will be skid marks all over the place, left by the rubber soles of Sinkers springing forth from the dark crevasses in which they lurk, desperate to latch onto you, suck you under and drag you down into the murky depths of failure.

These bitter losers are everywhere and can be a most elusive enemy, patrolling often undetected off the shores of Fat City with their periscopes up. They come in many guises, often appearing as allies and friends. Do not be suckered in by them, their 'help' can be deadly. 'Sticks and stones may break my bones but words won't ever hurt me' is lovely but simply not true. Their sinking thinking can be devastatingly damaging if taken on board; it is likely to slip deep into your incredibly receptive subconscious and grow into the deadly Arthritic Mountains, a range of man-made summits found only in people's own minds. To their poor, deceived victims these peaks appear to be impassable, and often hold them back for the rest of their 44.4s, their dreams sunken without trace.

To help you spot Sinkers, you may notice that when giving you advice they use a lot of N'T words: 'you can't', 'don't', 'mustn't', 'wouldn't', 'shouldn't...' etc., etc. If they do this, then try a simple litmus test on them by telling them just how great life is for you and how excited you are about the future. If they are genuine Sinkers, your good news will be a breath of foul air to them. Look closely behind their game-show-host smiles and you should notice the colour of their complexions change to a rather 'off', nauseous green. With their true colours revealed, you may also detect an odd smell that may bring back not-so-fond memories of Grandma's boiled sprouts as they open their mouths and say 'I'm really pleased for you.'

Tip: Look upon the little N'T comments of these disciples of the pear shape as positive pointers that you're on the right track. When they tell you that you can't do something, take it as an absolute guarantee that you certainly can.

Dodge the BLOATERS

BLOATERS are Boasting, Lazy, Obnoxious And Tediously Egotistical, Reptilian Saddos.

They are absolutely full of it! They never listen, take advice or practise and yet seem to have all the answers in the Universe. They have degrees in hindsight and spend their time spurting out and imposing their opinions on anyone who'll listen. Don't get taken prisoner by them; friendly faces are flypaper to BLOATERS. Don't give these bodysnatchers any chance to engage you, give them the slightest of openings and you'll come away feeling even more in the dark, confused and as though you've wasted years of your life. I would even suggest that a fair percentage of alien abductions could be put down to these absurd time bandits, with a great number of those people missing inexplicable chunks of time and genuinely believing they have been abducted by aliens, not realizing that they have in fact been the victims of Black Hole BLOATERS.

Listen out for anyone dispensing the following non-stop verbal slurry: 'Let me tell you... take a tip from me... If I were you... when I started off... the way I always look at it... when I was at your level... I did it the hard way... I put my success down to... as I always say... what always works for me... in my book... mark my words... should have listened to me... what you should have done is... I knew that would happen... been there, done that... I've met them... seen it all before... but much bigger and better than you... I could tell you a few things... enough about me... what do you think of me?'

Tip: If you should find yourself in close proximity to a BLOATER, just bear in mind that opinions are like farts; everyone likes their own. If you do begin to get the feeling that you are about to be taken hostage by them, try looking a little psychotic and deliberately twitch your head every time they look across at you.

Overtake Molasses Man

Molasses Man is a sweet but slow person burdened by the beliefs of others. Crawling along in the inside lane of life, these people are more of a potential hazard than an enemy. Try and avoid getting hemmed in by these well-meaning folk; when you see them it's time to check your mirror, put your foot flat to the floor and show them your tail pipe.

Jump the Head Treads

Head Treads really are the cream of the crap, they are the saddest and most insecure of all the enemies. Living on the outskirts, they are the 'ladder pullers' of Fat City. Having only made it into town themselves through luck, brown nosing, toadying and knife throwing, they have become closet members of the 'Keep Fat City Free of Real Talent' campaign in a pathetic attempt to guard the entrances and keep Fat City to themselves. These shallow and selfish individuals know deep down that they are devoid of both skill and ability. Terrified of being exposed for what they really are, they poop themselves whenever anyone more capable than them appears on the scene.

In contrast the long-term residents living in the centre tend to be welcoming of other people's success and achievements because they themselves have talent in abundance – so much so that they can afford to share it around with others.

As the self-styled door minders of Fat City, Head Treads take advantage of their positions of authority to hold others back and keep standards down. To do this they depend heavily on others paying too much respect to their no-entry-sign judgements, using them as stop bombs in a desperate bid to halt Fat City travellers in their tracks. Dropping them down from on high on anyone they see coming up the ladder, they live in the desperate hope that their judgements will never be questioned or challenged.

Typical Head Tread Poses

ENEMY ALERT:
If you have recently encountered any of these enemies, or if you have any knowledge about others not mentioned here and would like to help in the fight against them, then please contact the Polar Bear Pirate Information Desk immediately. Any information received will be treated in the strictest confidence.

No-entry-sign judgements include the likes of 'needs to keep head down... walk before they can run... early days yet... lot to learn... lacks experience... yet to prove... needs to work on... not been exposed to real pressure... the jury's still out... good, but... flash in the pan... different at this level... questions still to be answered... the real test will come when... long way to go yet... they come, they go... seen them crash and burn... doing a great job in current role... seem quite happy where they are... YOU'RE NOT COMING IN!'

Your Allies

Often appearing in many guises, shapes and sizes – and found in some of the most unlikely places – are any number of allies who, if you play your cards right, will make your passage to Fat City considerably easier. Not only will they help you root out your enemies, they will fight your corner and free you up to navigate your way forward.

BE AWARE OF PINEAPPLE PEOPLE

Pineapple People have the misfortune – and, at times, perhaps fortune – of being born looking as though they're fresh out of scare school. As a result these incredibly deceptive people invariably get mistaken for enemies of some sort and are avoided at all costs by those who are quick to make rash assumptions. Despite their spiky appearance they are actually incredibly sweet under-neath, you just have to get to know them and they have to come to trust you. If you do give them a little extra time Pineapple People usually make fantastically loyal friends and firm allies.

Some even turn out to be undercover Polar Bear Pirates. This being the case, it may well transpire that every time you've seen them on previous occasions they had been deliberately looking a little odd, because unbe-known to you there'd been a BLOATER about.

 Are there any scary-looking people that you have always avoided? If you gave them a bit more time might they possibly turn out to be Pineapple People or even plain-clothes Polar Bear Pirates?

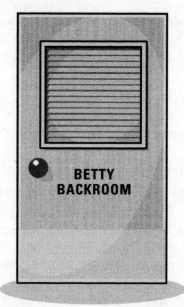

Betty Backroom

Don't mess with Betty Backroom, the loyal, caring, dedicated team treasure and keeper of sanity. The Bettys of this world get things done, sort things out and generally keep the ship on course. These limelight-shunning, unsung heroines are the archetypal linchpins who hold teams together in good times and bad. If you're ever in need of help or sound advice, Betty B should be your first port of call.

Non-political, independent and unphased by rank or title, Betty Backrooms speak their mind, can smell 'tonsil manure' a mile off and – because of an extremely well-developed sense of justice – are not afraid to go into battle to defend those in need. Indeed, anyone attacking one of 'Betty's People' without good cause either has a death wish or simply hasn't had the unforgettable 'deep joy experience' of having crossed her before.

You see, Betty Backrooms possess the kind of immense inner strength that has been forged from many years of experience – and, quite often, a fairly well-hidden but quite remarkable private and professional life. In fact, it would probably be worth betting that the 'early to bed' Bettys that most of us think we know have had strong links with the upper echelons of Fat City. It's even possible that she still has some influence there with today's movers and shakers. There can certainly be little doubt that Betty will be regarded with nothing less than the utmost respect by those seemingly whiter-than-white characters who, over the years, have come to view Betty as the trusted guardian of the keys to their own skeleton closets. Never, ever, underestimate the power of Betty!

If there are any slight criticisms to be made of these stalwart characters it is that their dry sense of humour can at times turn into breathtaking bluntness. As a result they may un-intentionally upset those they are trying to help. Old hands who have seen the comings and goings of many over the years, Betty Backrooms are also naturally suspicious of change and don't instantly warm to newcomers. It is highly likely that it will take a good deal of patience and determination to get them on your side. But it's well worth the effort, for if you succeed you will discover that you have one of the staunchest and deadliest allies walking beside you on your journey to Fat City. You merely have to remember three things when dealing with Ms B:

- **Be completely straightforward and open with her at all times.**

- **Utilize her vast store of experience and encourage her full involvement in any project you undertake.**

- **Do not be afraid to stand up to her. As well as finding Molasses Man highly irritating and viewing Neg Ferrets, Sinkers and BLOATERS with equal disdain, Betty also has a pathological loathing of woolly wimps and crawly sycophants.**

One final but vital piece of advice hinges on that thorny issue: respect. Getting a Betty Backroom to buy into you is one thing, gaining her respect is another – and it is something that won't happen overnight. In short, it will take time no matter who you are, where you've been or where you're going!

'Head down, arse up, lay bricks' – the daily mantra of any self-respecting Betty.

PUPs – Potential Unhatched Players

Every day hundreds of new PUPs enter the workplace, eager tail wagers who are desperate to learn, keen to please and brimming over with enthusiasm. After years of containment these PUPs are simply bursting with expectation for, at long last, they have in their sights newfound independence and a level of freedom they've never before tasted.

These hungry PUPs simply *ooze* potential but as yet have never really had the chance to realize it for themselves, let alone develop it. However, whether or not they fulfil this promise will largely depend on their new environment and the attitudes of those around them.

There are several likely outcomes for emerging PUPs:

- If conditions are just right, they will hatch out almost immediately and begin making their way to Fat City with other jubilant 'off-the-leash' escapees. *But,*

- Sadly, the vast majority of PUPs remain unhatched and end up feeling more and more frustrated and unfulfilled. They diligently work away in the hope that one day the right opportunity will present itself and they will be free to step out of the shadows and into the limelight.

- Another unfortunate possibility is that they may never have a chance to come into their own because they'll be gobbled up by the Neg Fraternity, who are always desperate to suck in and sign up any vulnerable little enthusiast. Indeed, the very presence of an exuberant PUP is certain to ruffle the feathers of BLOATERS, and their fresh and innovative ideas will act like a red rag to Sinkers and Neg Ferrets. The all-time favourite Neg Comment to a PUP has got to be: 'You won't be saying that when you've been here as long as I have!'

- By far the most tragic thing that can happen to a PUP is that they will become a victim of PUP-napping. This kind of corporate abuse, which drives PUPs out of teams by burying them alive and crushing their expectations, is usually carried out by a particularly jumped-up junior manager. These former PUPs turned Corporate Abusers were once the victims of similar bullying tactics and feel it is only right and fair to keep up the tradition by dishing out the same type of misery they had to endure. Too often, this kind of crime goes unreported, and many Corporate Abusers are free to roam the corridors of organizations, undetected and ready to gag – even murder – the talent of tomorrow.

Many organizations waste time and money looking out for new talent instead of investing in the rich seam of gifted people already available to them. If they only bothered to look under their own patios from time to time, they might just discover that, lying dormant and unfulfilled in their own back yard, are any number of PUPs – all bubbling away just under the surface and screaming out for a chance to prove themselves.

In contrast to this short-sighted behaviour, Polar Bear Pirates regard it as a primary duty to hatch out existing potential. They know that if they are going to help any PUP develop into an effective team player, the PUP will need strong support, bucketloads of encouragement and a little space to grow in. Polar Bear Pirates also know that if they want to continue to build an effective team around them, they must cultivate their own home-grown talent in a breeding ground that draws out the very best in people and allows individual characters to shine through.

Essential
Polar Bear
Pirate Packing

IF YOU ARE TO HAVE ANY HOPE OF
SURVIVING THE TREACHEROUS ROAD TO FAT CITY,
I STRONGLY RECOMMEND THAT YOU TAKE WITH
YOU, IN THE LARGEST POSSIBLE QUANTITIES,
THE FOLLOWING SIX BASIC ESSENTIALS:

DIY BELIEF • DOER • BALLS • ENTHUSIASM
HUMOUR • ASK RACKETS

DIY Belief

If you don't believe in yourself you will turn out never to have existed. Belief is a fundamental and absolute must for getting anywhere. At Oxford on 6 May 1954 Roger Bannister was the first person ever, in our entire history, to run a recorded mile in under four minutes. For years the Neg Ferrets and Sinkers had been saying that no one would ever do it, and BLOATERS by the bucketful had been dining out on their commonly held opinion that the human body wasn't up to it and that the mind would surely suffer some sort of overload from passing through the impassable four-minute barrier. It took just 3 minutes and 59.4 seconds for this mythical barrier to be smashed and for the Neg Fraternity to be sent scuttling back to the holes from which they had crawled, with the sonic boom from this 'impossible' breakthrough ringing in their ears.

Roger Bannister's astonishing achievement is of course widely known throughout the world today. What is far less well known, but is in my opinion equally remarkable, is that the dust on his spikes had hardly had time to settle before over three hundred other runners had followed in his illustrious footsteps within just a couple of years. There was nothing stopping them; this particular Arthritic Mountain didn't exist any more, it had been blown away by belief.

There are two types of belief. There is the extremely rare DIY Belief – Do It Yourself Belief which unfortunately only a few special people ever seem to have – and there is the far more abundant second-hand belief which everyone else gets for free after a person with DIY Belief has been along.

When once asked to explain his incredible feat and the art of record breaking, Roger Bannister answered, 'It's the ability to take more out of yourself than you've got.'

1954: A bad year for the BLOATERS

Doer

Probably the most basic and at the same time the most commonly lacking of abilities.

One thing that I've noticed in all the successful people I have ever met, whether they're in business, sport or entertainment, is that once they've thought things through, they get on with it. They are all doers, they are proactive people, they keep busy, moving and most importantly they keep on delivering. And not just when the surf's up, that is not just when everything is rocking along, but when things are down and there is no surf to pick them up and carry them. At the other end of the success scale, in depressingly large numbers, are the Y-fronts. They are full of promises, giving it the big Yes all the time; they have more front than Vegas but when it comes down to it, they never deliver – probably because they're just pants.

Thinking is dangerous. You plan and plan what you are going to do, then at some stage the talking has to stop and you have to leap over the gap between planning and action – in other words, you have to get on with it. This is the point when most people, along with their plans, become fatally unstuck because they forget to shut their minds, leading to them slowing down, stalling and falling straight into this deep and deadly gap. They slow down because with their minds open they are still thinking about other people's opinions. All those sinking thinking comments made by Sinkers over the years come flooding back up into the forefront of their minds and swamp them.

Someone once described the mind as being like a parachute in that it only works when it's open. This is absolutely true, but a parachute is designed to slow you down. It is crucial to have your mind open at the vital planning stages, but at the gap stages anything that slows you down is the last thing you need.

OPEN MIND: PLAN: SHUT YOUR CHUTE: MIND THE GAP!

Balls

Over the years a lot of people have assured me that they have the balls to succeed.

Many have gone to great lengths trying to persuade me, usually in bars, just how big their balls really are. They swear that to reach their dreams they are prepared to do and go through almost anything. You can therefore imagine my frustration and bitter disappointment when the majority of these well-meaning souls come across the first fluffy hurdles on the road to their dreams and collapse in inconsolable, gibbering heaps.

Maybe it's because they had their beer goggles on when telling me, or maybe it's because they haven't got the slightest clue as to what having real balls is all about. Faced with daunting hardship and with the heat turned up, a few people become rock solid – the further back they get pulled the higher they get catapulted – whilst the rest take on the shape and consistency of a dropped ice-cream.

When I think of balls I think of a handful of people including an amazing lady called Wilma Rudolph. Wilma was born prematurely into an extremely large and very poor family on 23 June 1940 in Clarksville, Tennessee. Having weighed in at only four and a half pounds she spent her first few years of life fighting off one illness after another, including scarlet fever and double pneumonia. When her left leg and foot started to become weak and deformed she was diagnosed as having polio and her mother was told that Wilma would never walk.

This news didn't seem to deter Wilma or her mother. Through sheer determination and with the support of her loving family Wilma began to fight back, using a relentless programme of physical therapy and battling day in, day out against a disease that she had been told had no cure. After years of gruelling pain, incredible hardship and desperately slow progress, her leg brace was finally binned: flying in the face of medical opinion, Wilma Rudolph could not only walk, she could run. After coming last in her first race at school, Wilma had the balls to carry on running and training to reach her dream.

In Rome, on 7 September 1960, Wilma Rudolph made her indelible mark in the sand. She became the first American woman to win three Olympic gold medals and entered into the history books as one of the greatest runners of all time.

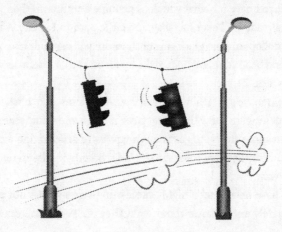

Enthusiasm

If all you have for what you do is genuine enthusiasm then you are already well over half-way down the path to Fat City. A few big dollops of pure grade-one enthusiasm will certainly give you a good head start and help make up for any other essentials you may lack.

When you're really enthusiastic, problems and obstacles don't seem to show their ugly faces as often and doors seem to open more freely; it's as though you were accelerating along on an unstoppable roller-coaster ride, bouldering them out of the way.

I have never met a highly successful person who is not passionately enthusiastic about what they do. People are drawn, like cats to kippers, to enthusiastic people. When you're with them you can feel the heat around them and you can hear them humming like dynamos; they light up rooms when they walk in and give off sparks of inspiration that ignite and rev the rest of their team.

If you are not enthusiastic about what you do then please don't expect anyone else to buy into what you're trying to achieve. If, however, you are enjoying yourself and want to start rubbing off some enthusiasm around the place, then please remember to tell your face.

In a team enthusiasm is more infectious than a bad cold and spreads almost as fast as the ugly butter (malicious gossip) peddled by the Neg Fraternity. If you do have anyone continuously raining on your party, keep going until you either turn them round or ride them out. If they won't buy into what you and the rest of your team are trying to achieve but appear to stick around specifically to undermine everyone's efforts, advise them to put a smile on it or give it big legs and take their traffic-warden faces, along with their bag of gloom, somewhere else. Give them a decent reference and with a bit of luck they'll get a job with the competition!

Believe you me, getting rid of them is always a good move, even if it leaves your team massively under-staffed. The last thing you need on your journey to Fat City is just one rotten apple giving off obnoxious and negative gases behind people's backs. The longer these poisonous people stick around, the more chance they will have of spreading their rot amongst the team.

Humour

This is a great weapon for disarming enemies and a wonderful advert for attracting allies.

Around our nervous systems are tiny tea bags, full of endorphins. Endorphin is abbreviated from endogenous morphine, which means a morphine produced naturally in the body. Endorphins remove stress and pain by blocking pain signals to the nervous system. The most effective of them all, beta-endorphin, has a wonderfully euphoric effect on the brain, making people feel relaxed and happy.

Endorphins or Big Es are incredibly powerful, they are readily available on tap around the clock, they're absolutely free and you don't get hangovers. Why waste hard-earned cash on less effective forms of chemically induced pleasure when you've got your own permanent in-house brewery and it's happy hour whenever you want?

It is widely believed that there are several ways of introducing drops of endorphin into someone's system under false pretences. These include physical exercise, eating sweets and chocolate, drinking tea and coffee, and laughing. Unless you intend to go for a run with everyone you meet or spend a small fortune on chocolate, cups of tea and coffee, your best way of releasing a few endorphins and getting people to say 'yes' to you is to put smiles on their faces.

 REASONS TO BE CHEERFUL: What ideas do you have for putting some big grins on a few faces?

Ask Rackets

Having the bottle to ask questions is a very useful thing to have; it helps to speed up your progress and slow down some of your enemies.

Besides being the obvious way of finding out information and showing an interest in people's favourite subject – themselves – a simple question can also be used as an effective attack or defensive counter-attack weapon. To do this, simply picture a question mark as a tennis racket: every time you ask a question, you whack a ball into someone else's court. This buys you time to think whilst they return your serve and puts you in control up at the net ready to volley or lob their reply.

Note: People who carry ask rackets around with them often give the impression of being more intelligent than they probably are.

Tip: Get your serve in first.

 Out of all these essentials which do you consider yourself to have the most of and which, if any, do you think you could perhaps do with a bit more of?

Look inside to find them

Whilst shopping around for these six necessities to take with you, you may notice that they are all fairly scarce in a surprisingly large number of adults, yet are all in abundance in the vast majority of young children. All of us were once brimming over with every one of the essentials on this packing list but somewhere along the line they seem to have got lost, stolen or knocked out of us. You may not remember but I'll bet that as a child you never stopped asking questions, you once believed in Father Christmas and the Tooth Fairy, you determinedly got on with things without thinking too much, you oozed enthusiasm and you got told off for giggling.

Lost Child

SO WHAT HAPPENED TO THE KID THAT COULDN'T WAIT TO WAKE UP AND SPRING OUT OF BED IN THE MORNING, TO THAT EXCITED LITTLE PERSON WHO KEPT ASKING IF THEY WERE HALF-WAY THERE YET AND WHO WAS SO DESPERATE TO BE THE FIRST TO SEE THE SEA? THE ANSWER IS SIMPLE: TO FIT INTO SOCIETY WE HAVE ALL BEEN CONDITIONED IN MANY DIFFERENT WAYS AND TO VARYING DEGREES AND EXTENTS BY OTHER PEOPLE'S NEEDS AND BELIEFS.

YOU WERE BORN WITH ALL THE NATURAL INGREDIENTS FOR SUCCESS IN ABUNDANT SUPPLY BUT AS A YOUNG CHILD, WITH LITTLE SELF-CONTROL AND NOT KNOWING ANY DIFFERENTLY, YOU WERE FAR TOO EXTREME IN YOUR USE OF THEM, USUALLY IN THE WRONG PLACES AND AT THE WRONG TIMES.

Your confidence once knew no bounds. If you fancied being an extremely noisy aeroplane or a motorbike in the middle of a busy department store, you'd be one. When your game was brought to an end by parents at the end of their tether, you'd think nothing of lying down on the floor and kicking your legs in the air in a wild tantrum. If you noticed that anyone had anything peculiarly odd about them, you probably wouldn't just point it out, you'd more than likely ask them right out and out loud why they had it.

BC (Before Conditioning)

For the sake of others this disruptive mini monster had to be reined in. Your behaviour had to change, you had to be conditioned and that child had to grow up.

The problem is that in most cases there was too much over-cooking in the conditioning process and far too many of our really useful natural ingredients got boiled away. Our fresh ideas became contaminated and our enthusiasm for life was burst by the beliefs of others.

We have all been held back on occasions from really going for it and at times from fully exploiting our own potential, thanks to the numerous left-over imaginary fences and barriers planted with good intention in our minds at school, to help make us better people and point us in the right direction.

Besides being built with our own welfare at heart many were doubtless erected with consideration given to the safety of others, as well as to keep us in line, stop us straying and – quite under-

standably – to help make some of our teachers' lives a little easier. Things like 'children should be seen and not heard' and 'they who ask don't get' may have served a purpose and been good for us during our early years, but still remain firmly in place throughout our

adult lives and form the subconscious foothills of our own Arthritic Mountain ranges.

Yes, we are indeed Prisoners of POO – People's Old Opinions. However, all is not completely lost. The child and all our vital ingredients are still alive and kicking somewhere deep down inside; we just have to realize it and release them.

Start acting your shoe size!

Having a childlike BC attitude is the most important qualification you must have if you want to be a Polar Bear Pirate and gain a substantial edge over the competition.

Go on, let the kid out! Release that excited bundle of energy that got shoved away under the stairs, fling open the door, brush off the cobwebs, jump in the odd puddle, have a pillow fight and blow some bubbles down your straw. Peer out from between your legs at an upside-down world, start looking at life through your own eyes once again and begin living it with the same zest and passion that you started out with. Do this and not only will you probably be pleasantly surprised by rediscovering the real you, you will also, without doubt, be amazed by what you are capable of achieving.

 When was the last time you did something incredibly silly but derived indecent amounts of pleasure from doing it?

Kid's stuff

As you step out beyond the old barriers, your new-found freedom will allow you to see things from completely new viewpoints and enable you to find opportunities that most 'grownups' wouldn't spot even if they were sprayed on their eyeballs.

The biggest secret behind the phenomenal success of Polar Bear Pirates is that they have the knowledge and experience of adults and the clear vision of children. Free from conditioning and other people's boring baggage they see no obstacles ahead of them and as a result they have an untarnished view of the way forward.

Their rediscovered BC mindsets enable them to see previously unnoticed openings from completely fresh angles and as they move forward, taking advantage of this, all their old confidence is re-released within them. They can go out and be audacious pirates once again, pirates who dare to create and steal opportunities from right under the noses of others.

Cuddly predators

A Polar Bear looks exceedingly cuddly, disguising the fact that it is one of the world's most dangerous predators and certainly one of its most aggressive babysitters. People who are Polar Bear Pirates also tend to be cuddly-looking on the outside but do not be fooled by their friendly, warm appearance for one moment. When it comes to playing the game they too are as much of a predator as their furry northern namesake, for underneath those loveable, huggable exteriors they are ruthlessly determined and focused on not just winning but on having a lot of fun along the way.

Cartoon time

Children's cartoons are often full of violence but no one really gets hurt; the story lines are uncomplicated as well as being great fun, the most unbelievable things happen all the time and the characters are all indestructible. PBPs view the way forward to Fat City with a cartoon attitude; to them nothing is taken personally, anything is possible and the most improbable things can be achieved. They adopt this attitude not only to make the game more fun and to keep things simple and in perspective, but also to speed up their progress by protecting themselves against becoming unfocused, bogged down or over-involved along the way with excess ego, emotion and politics.

Thumbs up to the critics

Being a PBP is very much about pulling revolvers on conventional thinking and spinning conventional attitudes 180 degrees. It's also very much about enjoying being the real you once again and being able to laugh at yourself before and after all the others do.

To become one of the game's real winners it certainly helps if you can adopt the refreshing attitude taken by PBPs towards criticism and rejection. PBPs regard both of these as trophies and accolades that are there to be collected in recognition of their attempts at reaching Fat City and as proof, not that they need it, of them actually doing something with their 44.4.

Problems are pregnant

PBPs love and embrace problems. In their eyes problems are beautiful things that are pregnant with opportunities; they just need fertilizing with a solution and the opportunity will be born. To do this you first of all have to be able to spot a problem, then identify the needs of others that are always twinned with it. If you can find a big enough problem that is common to a lot of people and then provide a solution, you're laughing.

What problems can you see that
may be ripe for inducing?

Problems are sticky things

As well as yielding up some great little results, PBPs also see
problems as being opportunities to glue people at all levels –
and from all sorts of diverse backgrounds – together. The
most solid of bonds and the longest lasting of relationships
are often created out of what initially appear to be the most
horrendous and unsolvable sticky situations.

Using and abusing Neg Ferrets

Problems are like eyelids in that you never get to see your own from the inside because you're up too close to them. Knowing this, PBPs listen to and make great use of the experts on the outside who are dedicated to pointing problems out: the Neg Ferrets.

If you are prepared to keep one ear open to their moans and complaints they'll eventually point you in the direction of some real nuggets. Don't have Neg Ferrets in your own team but at the same time, don't be nasty to Neg Ferrets in your competitor's teams; humour them and keep them close, you never know, they could find your passport to Fat City. If they do, you can either continue putting up with them, just in case they unwittingly point out another gem, or you can kick them, along with their attitudes, into touch with the same speed and relish with which you would dispose of a no-longer-required shopping trolley.

Can you think of any Neg Ferrets in your competitor's teams that may be worth some serious abuse?

ESCAPE TO THE OUTSIDE LANE

IF YOU ARE SICK OF FEELING HEMMED IN, IF YOU'RE
FED UP WITH THE SAME OLD VIEW OF SOMEONE
ELSE'S REAR, IF YOU'VE HAD ENOUGH OF PICKING
UP PUNCTURES FROM THE DEBRIS OF OTHERS AND
IF YOU'RE THOROUGHLY FRUSTRATED BY YOUR LACK
OF PROGRESS THEN YOU NEED TO GET SOME REVS
UP, PULL OUT OF THAT LORRY LANE AND GET SOME
BREEZE ON YOUR KNEES IN THE OUTSIDE LANE.

TO HELP THEM MAINTAIN THEIR SPEED AND STAY IN
THE OUTSIDE LANE PBPS USE THE FOLLOWING:

Remote control

The sooner you realize that it is just a game and that the barriers in your way are purely make-believe, built in the main by well-meaning and tired teachers, the quicker you will be able to lighten up and adopt the PBP cartoon attitude. This will not only help to protect you from taking things personally, it will also help you stay in the outside lane by giving you the confidence to step outside yourself from time to time, take a look at yourself and see the quickest way forward from a spectator's point of view.

 CHECK YOUR MIRRORS: If you want to get a better insight into how others view you then you may want to complete the PBP Questionnaire.

Sonar

'If you can keep your head when all about you are losing theirs, then you probably don't have a very good grasp of the situation around you.'

Anonymous PBP

If you are going to start travelling at high speed along the road to Fat City then it is vital that you are more alert than ever to your surroundings and any potential dangers that may lie ahead. Equally important is the need to have a stronger than ever sense of awareness of other travellers and an idea of where they're coming from.

SONAR is a wonderful piece of kit to possess. If you really do want to survive in the outside lane and vastly improve your chances of success, I'd strongly recommend you use it.

SONAR stands for Sounding Out Needs And Responding. If only a few people have the nerve to ask probing questions, then even fewer have the ability to really listen to the answers they receive and make good use of them.

Unfortunately far too many people think that they are strong communicators because they believe they have the gift of the gab; but with their transmit buttons permanently stuck in the on position they are unable to ever receive anything. PBPs know that good communication is all about understanding, which can only be achieved if you are in a position to receive in the first place.

One of the key things that make modern submarines so brilliantly effective compared with older subs is that they have SONAR. They use it to continuously ask searching, probing questions of their surroundings, listening intently for any potential threat and taking in vast amounts of information. When it comes to launching an attack they are precise and devastatingly deadly.

PBPs use SONAR not only to gain awareness of the state of

play around them but also to home in and lock onto the needs of others so they can support, work with, lead, motivate and influence them with far greater effect. SONAR is fundamental to effective teamwork and is vital for anyone looking for success in any business. Top sales people are SONAR Sales People, listening to and providing solutions that meet their clients' exact requirements, and all great leaders are SELLs (SONAR Effective Leading Leaders), in tune with their people and getting the very best out of them by responding to their individual needs.

A note here on TOEs: PBPs listen out especially carefully for TOEs, those tiny but telling Tag On Extensions that people frequently mutter and add on to the end of their answers – and which often lead to them putting their foot firmly in it!

How highly do you think others rate you as a SONAR communicator?

Beds

Big Exciting Dreams are essential in inspiring us to reach Fat City, to get us going and to keep us going with something to look forward to around the corner. They are wonderful things to have but will remain only dreams unless we work out the direction and steps we have to take to make them come true. If we don't, we'll just become one of the millions of Jellyfish People drifting with the flow, hoping that one day we will discover a magic lamp, give it a good rub and some bizarre, fashion-unconscious person will pop out and grant all our wishes. Forget it, the chances of this happening are considerably less than being beheaded by a Frisbee. What we need to do is start popping some SMUGs!

 What's your biggest BED?

Teaspoons of SMUGs

Small Unseen Goals are tiny personal goals that will help keep you on track to your BEDs. For them to work you must keep them really small and hidden away from the rest of the world, especially from Sinkers. I call them SMUGs because when you start to achieve them, despite their size, it's the same feeling as wetting yourself in a dark suit: you get a lovely warm feeling inside but no one really notices. Many people fail to achieve their dreams because they get too greedy and expect big, instant success. They either make their path along the way too steep with over-ambitious goals or they are unrealistic with their timescales. As a result they end up throwing in the towel, feeling hopeless, depressed and at times disliking themselves.

The key to avoiding this negative and self-destructive feeling of failure is to start and keep on enjoying the addictive taste of success by feeding yourself regular teaspoon-sized drops of achievement. Keep the tablespoons in the drawer; stick with the teaspoons and you'll avoid an awful lot of disappointment.

Get bubble wrapping

Lay down a path littered with SMUGs that are so easy to break that it's like walking on bubble wrap. You will be amazed at the immense amount of pleasure and self-satisfaction that you will derive from popping your SMUGs along the way, no matter how small they are.

For example, say your dream is to be a marathon runner. You remember that at school you used to do five-mile cross-country runs; however, you seem to have forgotten that since leaving school the only running you've ever done is to get out of the rain. The very first day you go out and try to push yourself through five torturous miles and end up hobbling home.

Would you feel good or would you feel disheartened with yourself, perhaps resigning yourself to the fact that since school things have obviously gone downhill in your fitness department? What would be the chances of you sticking at it and eventually reaching your Fat City?

However, suppose you went out for the first time and only did a slow mile, despite the fact that you probably felt capable of running much further. Then how would you feel after you'd got back and had a nice shower? If you did this just twice a week to start with and then, when ready, moved on to more and more SMUGs that together gradually built up over a pre-planned period of time, the chances of you achieving your BED would be vastly increased.

A Fat City road map

If you want to continue enjoying that tingly warm sensation from SMUG popping over sustained periods of time, it's probably wise to be prepared for some of life's many unforeseen diversions which are completely out of your control by having one or two alternative routes up your sleeve. PBPs draw up their own in-head Fat City road maps, plotting out a couple of optional B roads just in case a calamity of cosmic proportions should happen to sweep away their first-choice path. As progress is made they update their maps continuously to help keep them ahead of the forever-changing circumstances around them.

If you do decide to make a map it is worth remembering that, like all maps, yours could be used against you if it were to fall into enemy hands. Once you've drawn up your map, whatever you do, never ever show all of it to anyone, always keep it slightly folded. No matter how lovely or helpful people may seem, there is always the slight but very real risk that maybe one day you'll find them in your way.

With this in mind, many PBPs also carry dummy decoy maps with them, specifically made up with the intention of deceiving enemies. There is endless joy to be had from pretending to drop your guard and exposing a dummy to those you know for certain are enemies, wrong-footing them and sending them off in completely the wrong direction.

A good decoy map can also be brilliantly effective in flushing out previously undetected enemies. An old favourite PBP trick is to deliberately let someone whom they suspect is a bit dodgy see a duff map and then start giving out signals and drip-feeding comments that imply that they are badly wounded, lost without power or in a very weak position. Having leaked their misinformation, hopefully into the right ears, all the PBPs have to do is sit back and wait to see who moves in for the kill.

What SMUGs do you need to get plotting and popping right now?

Belief thermals

Bursting through your SMUGs on a regular basis will make you not only more motivated but increasingly addicted to keeping on going because you are continuously achieving something, enjoying little tasters of success and most importantly feeling good about yourself. As a result you step into a belief thermal. The more you do the better you become and the more you enjoy it, so the more you do it and the more your belief rises, riding on the back of the heat from your activity. A whole new positive chain reaction is kicked off inside you, leading to increased confidence and the enthusiasm to go out and achieve even more. Almost without even realizing it the norm in your mind is on the move, the view is improving and what was once just a BED is fast becoming reality as you surf and soar higher and higher.

Please note that you can go down as well as up in a belief thermal. I'll give you a couple of examples:

You feel overweight, and it depresses you. The more depressed you get, the more you trough out; the more depressed you get, the more you graze and the more you chub up. You feel tired so you spend the weekend sleeping; this makes you feel more tired so you laze around dozing on the sofa. This makes you feel even more tired so you go to bed, but you can't get to sleep because you feel too tired. When you get up on Monday morning you're completely spanked.

What, between 0 and 10,000 feet, would you estimate your current altitude to be?

Secrets of Your Mind

YOUR BRAIN IS A SERIOUS PIECE OF HARDWARE THAT IS CAPABLE OF RUNNING NUMEROUS MULTI-FUNCTION APPLICATIONS AND SENDING AND RECEIVING MILLIONS OF MAILS ALL AT THE SAME TIME. FAR MORE COMPLEX, HOWEVER, IS THE SOFTWARE THAT RUNS ON IT. YOUR MIND IS COMPLETELY UNIQUE TO YOU AND IS PROBABLY ONE OF THE MOST SOPHISTICATED SOFTWARE PACKAGES AVAILABLE IN THIS UNIVERSE. IT HAS BEEN FULLY CUSTOMIZED AND EXTENDED THROUGH EXPOSURE TO VARYING ENVIRONMENTS AND YOUR OWN PERSONAL EXPERIENCES. AS YOU MOVE ON THROUGH LIFE IT CONTINUES TO UPGRADE AND CHANGE; ITS CAPABILITIES ARE UNLIMITED AND, PROVIDED YOU ARE AWARE OF THE ENEMIES DISCUSSED EARLIER AND THE VIRUSES MENTIONED LATER, ITS POTENTIAL APPEARS TO BE INFINITE.

To help save vast amounts of time and to protect themselves from turning fruit loops, PBPs don't attempt for one moment to try and fathom out the inner workings of their own minds. This, to them, would be as absurd as having an urge to take the back off a television to see how it works, the truth being that they wouldn't really care if they discovered it to be powered by a couple of happy hamsters running around on wheels. Trivial technical detail involving such wonderful terminology as oscillating flux capacitors is not only miraculously yawn-inducing but also completely irrelevant as far as PBPs are concerned.

When it comes to their own minds, the only thing that really matters to them is the fantastic range of capabilities they have to offer and how those capabilities can be maximised to benefit them and gain any advantage they can in their race to reach Fat City. To do this they only have to know a few basics, and it should certainly help you to progress faster and further in the long run if at this point we pause for a while and take a quick look at the mind from a PBP point of view.

The mind as understood by PBPs

Your mind is split into two areas, the big boss hard disk and the little boss floppy. By far the biggest and by light years the most important is your big boss hard disk, a massive virtual disk which is about the size of your average four-bed detached. It is immensely powerful and its main role as your silent governor is to control all your systems completely, including physical functions and thought processes. It discreetly takes care of business even whilst you sleep.

It has been continuously looking after you and catering for your every need, unnoticed, non-stop around the clock, without pay and without any breaks, since you were in the womb. Right now it's controlling and running everything from your breathing (hopefully!) right down to your blink rate. I would hazard a guess that apart from now being suddenly aware of your breathing you probably won't be able to stop blinking for the next couple of pages!

As your protector your big boss hard disk is always on guard against potential danger and will soon alert you if and when it feels it needs to make you aware of any possible hazard or draw your attention to anything it knows could be of specific interest to you. For example, you might start thinking about getting a cat and almost as soon as this thought enters your head, you start noticing cats all over the place.

The key to its power and continued success on your behalf

is its ability to gather information and intelligence. It works in a sense like a flight-box recorder and, if the conditions are right, it is capable of taking in millions of bite-sized chunks of information from the world around you, all in a matter of seconds.

Picture files

All this information is saved in full-colour 3D picture format in files deep inside your hard disk. These files form the fundamental foundations and building materials on which your beliefs, perceptions, attitudes, habits, characteristics and personality have been created and continue to be built, based on pictures of past experiences.

Whilst you are reading this your mind modem is converting the words into pictures derived from every one of your previous experiences. If an original picture doesn't exist or can't be found in your files, your hard disk will kindly oblige by creating and generating a new one for you and then displaying it in your imagination.

Old favourites

The more often you do something, whether you are doing it well or cocking it up, the more pictures you will have of doing it and the more likely you are to do it again.

What do you wish you had more pictures of yourself doing?

Access all areas?

Working on behalf of your big boss hard disk, but only a part-time basis, is your lightweight, little boss floppy. Acting in its very limited capacity as a sidekick and runner, its main job is to look after the relevant but relatively small amounts of practical information used by you on a day-to-day basis. Being typical of those in possession of only a tiny amount of authority, your floppy likes to give the impression that it wields a lot more clout than it really does and as a result the vast majority of people are often fooled into mistaking this little boss for their big boss.

Those who make this mistake, or genuinely believe that by accessing just their floppy they will bring about profound changes, are labouring under a massive misapprehension. They are extremely unlikely to ever walk the streets of Fat City, let alone take up residence there. If you are serious about making real, lasting changes, it is vital that you gain access to your hard disk and don't waste too much time talking to its sidekick. This is why hypnotists don't muck about with it; they cut out this over-hyped middleman and talk directly to the decision maker.

I wasted years chatting to the sidekick. I used to smoke

forty cigarettes a day and almost every other day I'd try to pack up; my attempts at stopping became a joke amongst my friends. I would keep on telling myself that I was mad to smoke and come out with all the usual clichéd stuff:

> 'It's killing me...
> It's a waste of money...
> I stink... I'm the only one
> out here in the rain...
> I'm an outcast!'

I didn't realize that these repeated complaints were futile because they were falling on the impotent ears of my rather pathetic floppy. I began to think all hope of kicking the habit had been lost and the very thought of being a life-long slave to the weed only seemed to fuel my addiction and increase my nicotine consumption.

My hard disk, being totally unaware of my new desire to change, was simply carrying on as normal, catering for my needs and assuming that I wanted to continue enjoying a good smoke. This is quite understandable as all the smoking-related pictures I held on file were of me deriving considerable pleasure from cigarettes.

I don't want to bang on about it but, believe you me, you can talk to your floppy until the cows drink milk. If you really want things done, talk to the big boss.

On my fortieth birthday I put into practice some basic self-hypnosis techniques that I'd been taught, gained access to my hard disk area and had a good look through some of my picture files. I bunged out all my old smoking pics and replaced them with new ones of me deriving similar pleasure from drinking copious amounts of fresh fruit juice and black coffee during the day, supplemented by the occasional glass of something slightly stronger after dark.

Without wishing to sound like a conceited ex-smoker, or be a bit of a BLOATER here, I feel I must say – with huge amounts of uncontainable smugness and immeasurable glee – that I haven't had or even wanted a cigarette since.

What old pictures could you do with chucking out and replacing?

Access for creativity

PBPs are highly imaginative and very creative individuals, often coming up with inspirational ideas and at times quite amazing solutions to the toughest of problems. Besides having the enormous advantage of being able to apply their childlike, unconditioned approach to problem solving, they also know how to utilize and explore to the full the immense creative capabilities of their big boss hard disk.

The 4Bs and Noddies

To open the door to your hard disk, gain access to your picture files and take advantage of its amazing capabilities, you need to do one simple thing, and that is – relax.

I'll bet the best ideas you have ever had came to you when you were in one of the 4Bs: Bed, Bog, Bath or Bar. These are the four most popular places where people get to unwind enough to be allowed access to an open-door hard disk. You can be struggling all day just to remember someone's name and just as your cheeks hit the pan, bingo! That elusive name suddenly jumps out at you from nowhere.

Out of the four, the bog and the bath are the two favourites for producing our best ideas because these are the two places where you are more likely to experience a Noddy.

A Noddy occurs when you relax just to the point when you

nod off for a few seconds and slip very briefly into your hard disk area, but return in the nick of time to remember and retain any fresh ideas you may have glimpsed whilst in there. The reason why you pop out so quickly is because, as your protector, your ever-alert, big boss hard disk is not going to allow you to doze right off whilst you are in a bath for obvious reasons of safety, and in a toilet, probably more than anything else, to save you from a potentially embarrassing situation. In both of these precarious predicaments it kicks you out, sounds the alarm and wakes you up.

However, if you are in bed it obviously won't see any real harm in letting you drop in for a much longer visit. This is fine, but your chances of remembering any bright ideas you may have had after dropping off for all that time will be greatly reduced. As for having a Noddy whilst in a bar, the problem here again is remembering it. It's sometimes hard enough remembering which bar you were in, let alone any awesome ideas you might have stumbled across whilst in there!

Out of the 4Bs, which is your favourite place for having bright ideas?

The art of the dunk

Over the years many highly celebrated and illustrious PBPs
have described their having mastered the art of the dunk as
being the key secret behind some of their most creative work.
To dunk is to deliberately dive into your hard disk area to find
ideas and solutions; in other words it's a premeditated, self-
induced, extended form of Noddy.

Like anything, being a top dunker takes practice. For a dunk to have any real chance of being successful you need to access your hard disk for a tad longer than normally permitted by a natural Noddy. The whole aim is not just to have a quick peep but to have a bit of a nose round whilst in there. Timing, as any experienced biscuit dunker will tell you, is crucial. Making a perfect dunk is all about staying in long enough to achieve your objective and pulling out in the nick of time just before everything melts away and drops off completely. This precise moment, beyond which there is no return, is known amongst regular dunkers as Point Plonk.

One particularly notable dunking method pioneered by Thomas Edison, and still used by PBPs today, is to sit late at night in a comfortable chair placed on a wooden floor whilst clutching in one hand, dangling strategically over the side of the chair, a couple of large ball bearings or marbles. The theory is that as soon as you begin to slide into deeper sleep and get near to Point Plonk your hand will release its contents and the noise will wake you up in time for you to grab and hang onto whatever inspirational nuggets you may have gleaned whilst in there.

How might it be possible for a good dunk to help you at this precise moment?

POP

When it comes to boosting their performance PBPs often use POP – Power Of Picture – to help gain that little extra that makes them extraordinary.

Our big boss hard disk communicates with and instructs our body to do whatever it wants it to do, dishing out its orders by again using 3D pictures. However, when it comes to receiving these pictures, our body isn't always the sharpest knife in the drawer and will believe any picture it is sent by the hard disk no matter whether it's real or a complete fake. If the boss says it's real, it's real as far as our body is concerned.

Knowing this, the boss likes to play games with our resting body during quieter periods and keeps it on its toes by deliberately sending out forgeries that it has created in our imagination. For example, you are dozing off on a train when you picture yourself suddenly rolling over the edge of a wall. You instantly wake up in a panic with your body really shaken up by it. Luckily you soon realize that you haven't rolled off anything and apart from the person next to you, whose shoulder your head has embarrassingly been resting on, no one else has noticed. This is your bored big boss having a laugh at the expense of your gullible body.

PBPs also take advantage of their bodies not being particularly streetwise. Without even getting out of a chair, you can do some very useful mental warm-ups in preparation for popping a few of your SMUGs. Again the key here is to relax but this time just enough to start vividly picturing yourself smashing your SMUGs. Really focus in on these positive pictures and hold them in your imagination for long as possible. As soon as your body starts to buy into them it will immediately begin to mobilize armies of its cells ready for action, then when it comes to popping your SMUGs for real you should find them just that little bit easier to do.

PBP formula:
RELAX + POP + DO = RESULT

 WAYS TO UNWIND: Do you know of any novel ways to help people relax in and out of the workplace?

TNTs –
The Difference

AT THE END OF THE DAY THE EXTENT OF
YOUR SUCCESS IN PLAYING THE GAME AND
REACHING FAT CITY WILL LARGELY DEPEND
ON HOW WELL YOU HAVE MASTERED
THE USE OF TNTs AND HOW AND
WHEN YOU HAVE DEPLOYED THEM.

Despite being tiny, TNTs are incredibly important. Many friendships have been won and lost through them, long-term marriages have broken up over them, wars have kicked off because of them and people have been inspired by them to climb mountains and sail oceans.

TNTs are the highly explosive Tiny Noticeable Things that we all spot about each other and which seem to either really please us or wind us right up, turning on occasions even the most placid and mild mannered of people into unrecognizable, raving, psychopathic lunatics.

TNTs have huge impacts

When it comes to information intake, your hard disk is exactly like a huge plankton hoovering whale in that it can digest vast amounts but only in millions of tiny bits. This is because all around the outside of the hard disk area is a honeycomb grille that is there to protect it from too much information overload. As a result, big things such as major news items don't sink in very quickly but little things, especially TNTs, have fast-track access.

Human nature being the way it is means that we all like to see things the way we want to see them, and that we therefore like to categorize our picture files. That's why it's annoying when you can't make up your mind whether you like someone or not, but they never give you an excuse to really get to hate them.

As we get older we gradually divide our files into two distinct types for the things we like and the things that we definitely don't like; in other words, we tend to pigeon-hole things a lot more. With our carefully categorized boxes in place we become primed to play a game of solo snap as we proactively look out for negative or positive TNTs that match up with the existing pictures in our boxes. For example, someone comes for a meeting with you wearing a nice dark suit and black shoes. All appears OK until he suddenly crosses his legs and exposes a tiny area of white towelling sock. Instantly there is an explosive impact in your mind as this TNT gets rocketed through your hard disk grille and straight into a file, probably somewhere in your 'wide boy' section.

Top 20 winders

The list of negative TNTs that really gripe people is endless, and obviously varies from person to person, but here are just a few of the most popular ones:

1. Loo seats left up
2. Drivers indulging in nostril caving whilst stationary at traffic lights
3. That sixth item in the basket of the person in front of you in a '5 items or less' queue
4. Cars that take up two spaces in full car parks
5. Apologizing to someone after they have just bumped into you
6. The use of finger gestures to draw imaginary inverted commas in the air
7. Clichéd motivational posters
8. People at the front of long queues who have a good old chin-wag with the only person serving
9. Those who answer their mobiles and tell the caller that they can't talk because they're on a train, but

who then proceed to chat loudly for the entire duration of your journey
10. Bright sparks in horror films who say 'let's go outside and investigate'
11. Dentists asking you questions whilst your mouth is jammed open and stuffed full of industrial sucking equipment
12. Hand towel machines that only allow you one stingy click's worth of grubby towel
13. The words 'you are held in a queue'
14. Lorries that cover up the signpost you've been desperately searching for
15. Those who try to sneekily read your newspaper whilst you're reading it
16. Handy ventilation shafts which are never working and that always lead our film heroes to the precise location that they are trying to reach
17. Receptionists with singing voices
18. Ignorant drivers who don't acknowledge your existence after you've pulled over for them
19. Politicians not answering the question
20. Politicians

OFF YOUR CHEST: What TNTs get you all cranked up?

TNTs please

Although often harder to see there are also positive TNTs that please people and are capable of making them feel good about themselves. Simple words such as 'thank you' seem to be becoming increasingly rare these days but, if used at the right time and said in the right way, can have surprisingly profound effects. It is these positive TNTs that PBPs know the value of and put to good use.

TNTs are free

Positive or negative TNTs make the difference between a fully booked, profitable hotel where guests don't mind paying that little bit extra and a cheap hotel that's half empty.

One of the busiest pubs I know is not popular for any other reason than the attitude of the staff who work there; they are what I call PHPs, Proactively Helpful People. They always go out

of their way to make anyone who goes in feel genuinely welcome and, probably without even realizing it, they use lots of simple, positive TNTs to great effect. They tend to remember first names, they seem to know everyone's preferred tipple and always take the time to say goodbye when you leave. These free but not over the top TNTs might be basic and appear to be glaringly obvious, but they certainly keep the tills busy.

I never cease to be amazed by the attitudes of those people working in client-facing roles who seem to regard customers and clients as some sort of inconvenience. I find it staggeringly unbelievable that I'm often made to feel as if I am an unwanted intrusion by so many shop assistants. All too often I feel that I'm doing a very good impersonation of the invisible man whilst waiting to be served, having at times almost to apologize for daring to interrupt their private conversations just to prove my existence.

I find it almost laughable when I go to check into a hotel and I'm greeted not by the friendly, charming, helpful person portrayed in the fabulously glossy brochure but by Hissy The Pissy Python who has a face like a spanked arse. What really takes the biscuit for me is when, having got past Hissy, I arrive in my room only to discover that the warm welcome I've been assured of is in fact an impersonal text message delivered to me via a television screen. Maybe the people at the top of some of these organizations are so busy developing their corporate image that they don't have the time to bother with their staff at grass roots level or to worry about incidental little things such as customers.

This, of course, is great news as far as PBPs are concerned, for the more 'Wet Mondays' there are working for their competitors, the easier it is for them to shine and the quicker they and their team will be arriving in Fat City.

 YOUR NOMINATIONS PLEASE: Would you like to nominate a PHP whom you feel deserves some recognition?

TNTs rev people's strides

I have seen on many occasions over the years people being motivated by free or very inexpensive things. I've witnessed people who drive extremely expensive cars fill up with petrol and complain that they've only been given three petrol vouchers instead of four, quite remarkable when you consider the billions of vouchers they have to collect just to get a two-slice toaster. I know of numerous highly successful people who have experienced pre-death rigor mortis from sitting through the most mind-numbingly boring of presentations just to get a T-shirt or a mug. Perhaps slightly disturbing is the number of people I have met who would be willing to take a drastic cut in salary just to have the word 'Director' or 'Partner' on their business card. What I have derived from these experiences is that you don't always have to throw money at people to motivate them.

A cautionary note:

In the workplace there is probably no better opportunity than an appraisal for TNTs to be effectively displayed to motivate – or de-motivate – what were previously quite happy people: 'Right, Julie, let's get on with it. I've got a golf lesson booked for five thirty.'

Pit stops

One of the best TNT motivators that has worked well for me and which is absolutely free is the Pit Stop. A Pit Stop equates to an hour off work. At the end of each day everyone in the team votes to award Pit Stops to members of their team whom they feel have worked especially hard or have done something outstanding. They are not, however, given out like sweets; on some days several may be awarded and on other days none at all. Team members save up these Pit Stops and use them when they need to take time off work. By using them you are highlighting success and rewarding people with their time for being productive in your time.

 What TNTs do you think you most commonly display to others?

TNTs produce memorable snapshots

Image these days, whether you like it or not, is of the utmost importance. The images of people, products and services seem to have become, in many instances, more relevant than what lies behind them. To realize the power of hype you need look no further than people paying to drink other people's old rainwater. Somewhere along the line fiendish marketing wizards have managed to completely transform the image of yesterday's rain and bottle it, making thirsty guzzlers around the world in their droves not only want to down it by the case but, at the same time, happily fork out hard-earned cash for the privilege of doing so. You only have to spell naïve backwards to begin to wonder if someone really is taking the piste.

Snapshot pictures leave behind the biggest and most lasting of images as well as the fondest of memories. You could have worked devotedly for the same company for forty years, seven days a week and not even taken a day off. Then, just as you stepped up to collect your thank-you gift at your leaving presentation there might accidentally squeak out from between your nervous butt cheeks an involuntary, but perfectly audible, single-note cloth cough. I guarantee that after forty years of loyal service that one crotchet of time would be the snapshot memory of you that everyone would not only keep, but also cherish and share.

Note: The most common snapshot favourite involves skirts being caught up in the back of knickers in very public places!

What snapshots will people
keep of you?!

Playing Together

YOU'LL PROBABLY FIND YOUR JOURNEY A WHOLE
LOT EASIER AND CONSIDERABLY MORE ENJOYABLE IF
YOU ARE ABLE TO SHARE THE UPS AND DOWNS
WITH A FEW OTHER PLAYERS.

PBPS ARE BY NO MEANS SOLITARY CREATURES
AND ALTHOUGH THEY ARE VERY ABLE PEOPLE,
CAPABLE OF GOING IT ALONE, THEY MUCH PREFER
TO TRAVEL WITH FRIENDS. BESIDES MAKING THE
WHOLE EXPERIENCE FAR MORE REWARDING AND
A LOT MORE FUN, THEY ALSO REALIZE THE HUGE
BENEFITS TO BE HAD FROM HAVING A FEW
LOYAL TRAVELLING COMPANIONS.

Hedgehog Heads and Dolly Teams

PBPs value above all else the people around them and the contributions made by them. They know that one of the keys to winning the game is to be able to get the very best out of others and to harness and fully utilize their individual characters, skills and talents. They understand that if people are relaxed and enjoying their work they are far more likely to be successful than those who are working in an unduly pressurized way. If people are constantly frightened of stepping out of line or of making mistakes their minds will become like frightened hedgehogs, clamming up into tight little balls. As a result of being continuously curled up tight they find themselves being denied hard disk access, their performance levels fall and, unsurprisingly, the number of sick days taken rises. Eventually the managers responsible for causing these prickly environments end up becoming even more authoritarian, turning into Sergeant Shout without even realizing it, and barking out orders all the time as they try to control what are now Zoo Teams, full of the animals they have created.

These restrictive environments stifle childlike vision, suffocate PUPs, drive out the free minded before they become RC'd (reconditioned) and leave the rest behind to become prime candidates for catching the Dolly virus. Inevitably Sergeant Shout's Zoo Team turns into a Dolly Team full of brown-nosed clones, all capable of licking their own eyebrows and possessing enough suck to suck start leaf blowers. Unless urgent action is taken, the team inevitably ends up as a Toilet Team, heading down the pan.

How could the environment where you are possibly be improved?

Spot-on DOT teams

The environment in which PBPs operate is extremely important to them, as they know that it can greatly influence their chances of ever seeing Fat City. As leaders they realize that their people will grow to reflect whatever environment they create around them. They know that they will only be able to bring out the best in people and get them to work to their full potential if those people are themselves having fun, accessing their hard disks and being positively challenged. If they themselves, as PBPs, are constantly being restricted from creating a SEE (Solution Enhanced Environment) they will take steps to change it. If they can't, they will move on to where they can be free to expand their own minds, to fully exploit their childlike qualities and have a fair crack at making it to Fat City with some other, more imaginative, folks.

PBPs like DOT (Diversity Of Thought) Teams. They know that the best way to reach Fat City is with a focused team of individuals, each bringing their own unique contribution to the table. A DOT team is a team that is absolutely spot on because each member is not only allowed but positively encouraged to be themselves, to be different, to say what they really think, to have an input and to bring to the team whatever it is they do best.

Lust

Another reason why DOT teams tend to be highly successful is because all the members, no matter what role they have, have respect for each other. They all support and inspire one another quite simply because between them, as a close knit team, they have loads of LUST.

PBPs love LUST. They seek out, build and enjoy relationships based on pure LUST (Loyalty, Understanding, Sharing and Trust) whenever and wherever they can, both in and out of work. They know, as team players, that the best way of developing LUST with those around them is by using their SONAR to understand and appreciate others and to communicate more effectively with them by sharing their visions and ideas around. As leaders they understand the importance of passing their visions up and down the line not only to provide their team with direction but, equally importantly, to give each and every member a sense of belonging to something rather special and of being very much a valued part of that special something.

Without doubt the easiest way for you to reach Fat City is to help those going with you to thrive and flourish by spreading a little LUST here and there. As you travel together, providing you all have your SONAR switched on, the LUST should gradually grow between you. The bigger it gets, the more you will all begin to pull together as an immensely powerful and effective spot-on DOT Team of unlike-minded individuals.

Which relationships could work better for you with a little more LUST?

WARNING: WATCH OUT FOR HITCHERS

Be wary of anyone who keeps using the old cliché 'there is no I in team'. It could well be that they are a hitcher looking for a free ride in your team, and that what they really mean is that they can't see an I in work. If someone in your team is persistently found to be guilty of freewheeling by fellow team members and continuously refuses to get pedalling then you have only one sensible option and that is to pick up some real speed, open the door and boot the work-shy freeloader out.

WANTED: Ideas for generating LUST, suggestions for creating more productive environments and any great team motivators you may have come across.

A Final Reminder

MOST PEOPLE APPEAR TO LIVE THEIR LIVES
ASSUMING THAT THEY ARE HERE INDEFINITELY ON
SOME KIND OF FREEHOLD BASIS. THEY MUST THINK
THAT THEY CAN AFFORD THE LUXURY OF BEING
ABLE TO SPEND THEIR TIME PONDERING ON AND
SCRUTINIZING THE SAME OLD MONOTONOUS
STUFF DAY IN DAY OUT.

They waste the only go they are ever going to get worrying unnecessarily about the most unimportant things and take themselves and all the irrelevant things in life far too seriously. Maybe if they knew the reality of their 44.4 short-term tenancy agreement they'd try and make more of their brief stay by focusing on the important, relevant and good things around them, leaving the glum side for the bottom-feeding Neg Fraternity to dwell upon.

Your time is your most precious commodity and it's becoming scarcer and more precious with every passing tick of your clock, so be careful not to squander it or let others steal it. It's also worth remembering, as you make your way along your chosen path to your Fat City, that it's your go and nobody else's, so don't go blowing it by trying to please everyone else all the time.

The time con

Despite time being the most precious of all things the vast majority of people seem to devote an awful lot of time to wasting it. They either spend it wishing it away by trying to fast forward on to potentially more exciting future events or they spend it rewinding back to memorable events in the past. The only time most people live for now is when they wake up five minutes before their alarm clock is due to go off on a cold, dark workday morning.

Time may be a human invention but it's certainly nobody's

friend. It loves to muck us about and frustrate us by speeding up when it thinks we are enjoying ourselves and slowing down when we are fed up, miserable or bored. If you are enjoying yourself at a party time seems to fly by but when you're freezing to death or getting soaked waiting just a few minutes for a taxi, those particular minutes can feel like a bad week.

There may be no way of hanging on to it but there is a way, if ever needed, of conning it into speeding up. When you next find yourself having to do a particularly scummy job like washing up a battle-hardened scrambled egg pan, just do what PBPs do in cases like this: take a long slow look over your right shoulder, put on the mother of all smiles, get stuck in and look like you're loving it!

FAFFing about time

Being a PBP is a lifestyle thing and PBPs value above all else their time spent with their family and friends. To ensure they get to enjoy enough of this quality time, PBPs proactively set aside specifically allocated periods of FAFF time (Family And Friends First time). Absolutely nothing, bar the most extreme of life-threatening emergencies, is allowed to encroach upon this most highly valued of all time. As well as

ensuring that they get to be with the most important people in their lives on a regular basis, setting aside FAFF time helps PBPs prevent their career and personal life becoming blended into one big mushy purée. It also helps keep them down to earth and completely refreshed for when it comes round to Fat City playtime.

When is your next FAFF time pencilled in?

Viruses

EVEN THE STRONGEST WILLED, MUCH LOVED AND
WELL MEANING OF FOLK CAN AT SOME STAGE
DURING THEIR CAREER BEGIN TO ACT COMPLETELY
OUT OF CHARACTER. WITHOUT EVEN REALIZING IT
THEMSELVES, THEY START TO DO ODD LITTLE THINGS
AROUND THE PLACE, THEIR BEHAVIOUR GRADUALLY
BECOMES A BIT MORE PECULIAR EACH DAY AND,
IF NOT HELPED IN TIME, THEY WILL BECOME
REGARDED AS SOMEONE ELSE WHO HAS
LOST THE PLOT.

For years these poor people have been shunned as workplace weirdos and their strange behaviour has in many cases been brushed under the carpet as 'stress'. It has only very recently come to light that many of them have in fact been the victims of previously unidentified but highly contagious viruses that have wormed their way into their heads, infecting and corrupting their hard disks.

URGENT APPEAL:
At the time of going to print,
only the following viruses had
been recognized. It is believed that
there are potentially hundreds, if
not thousands, more out there. Your
assistance is desperately needed now
in identifying and highlighting any
viruses you may be aware of. If you
know of any antidotes or vaccines
that could possibly give a poor victim
somewhere a chance of saving their
career before it's too late, we'd very
much like to hear from you. Please go
without delay to the PBP Info Desk.
Thank you.

Albert And Victoria

The oldest of all the viruses, particularly rife amongst insecure managers. It gives its poor, misguided victims an unbelievable compulsion to go forth and build empires.

Anteater

This common virus is a member of the Micro Mind family of viruses. It attacks people's vision, making them short-sighted, and renders them incapable of taking in the bigger picture.

Badge Boys

Seems to give lonely and uninteresting people an overriding compulsion to openly display labels and stickers as proof of their membership of various saddo clubs, societies and organizations.

Betamax

Quite extraordinary, gives its victims the power of hindsight and turns them into monotonous post-event experts with an overwhelming compulsion to keep rewinding.

Big Chum

Attacks unfocused individuals and is most common amongst weak managers. Brings about certain failure by making them feel like they have to please everyone all the time.

Bob's

Bob's virus seems to target itself invariably at under-performing managers, bringing them out in cold sweats and causing them to engage in bricklaying activities around their own departments.

Card Tarts

Targeting itself specifically at the Norms, this mocking virus gives its carriers an unstoppable desire to give off the impression of Fat City residency by causing them to flash in public, at every possible opportunity, their entire collection of credit cards.

Daniel's Derriere

Highly irritating, causes people to keep disappearing up their own rear.

Dolly

A sadly all too common one that for some unknown and mysterious reason makes team members want to be exact clones of their boss. Obvious symptoms are brown rings forming around the nasal area. Usually causes considerable nausea to those around them.

Gob Lobs

This curious virus turns up the volume control on its victims' voices but at the same time muffles their hearing. Those who suffer from it seem to feel an overwhelming desire to hold conversations across rooms.

Graft Grommet

A strange one, turning those infected with it into closet masochists. People suffering from it tend to go out of their way to deny their love for their work despite being totally obsessed with it.

Grindstone Cowboy

Related to the Graft Grommet virus but having almost exactly the opposite effect. Victims of it are prone to continuous boasting about their workload. They tend to spend long hours at the office but show very few signs of actually ever doing any work.

Hide And Seek Champions

An odd one, forcing people to exaggerate their job titles to make them sound grander and more complicated than they really are so that they can then either hide behind them or merely intrigue people.

Igloo

Dangerous and sadistic, it lulls those it infects into having a nice warm feeling of security and encourages them to feel quite at home just at times when they are unwittingly on very thin ice.

I'm Just

A confidence sucker that makes people infected with it put themselves down all the time. Victims feel forced to begin their reply to any questions asked about their role with the words 'I'm just...'

Jaffa Gaffa

By far the most bizarre of all known viruses. It only seems to manifest itself in managers with inflated egos. It may sound absurd, but it makes them believe that they really are a cake amongst biscuits.

London Sparrow

Common to those who never really do anything themselves. The symptoms are large amounts of twitter and poop. If not dealt with early, its carrier is highly likely to develop into a full-blown Y-front.

Lucans

It causes those it corrupts to frequently disappear just when there's work to be done or a problem to be sorted. The extended version has a tendency to bring on sickness symptoms on a regular basis, particularly on Mondays and Fridays.

Overhead

An unbelievably common virus that makes its victims feel they are not really working unless they are in a meeting.

Reagan's

Often fatal as it takes over its victims' minds and makes them believe that they really should give up a perfectly good career and take up politics on a full-time basis.

Soap Sods

Brings on a sudden need in those it infects to make rash and at times weird excuses in order to clear off early and secretly watch TV soaps. Although sounding well informed on the soap front, its victims have a tendency to deny all knowledge of ever having actually watched a single episode.

Spoon Benders

Very nasty, cons its victims into genuinely believing that they possess supernatural mental powers and that they can get results just by sitting back and willing things to happen.

Velcro Man

Attacks people who lack confidence in achieving the task before them. As a result they jump on any opportunity to hook into anything but the job in hand. Common symptoms are a desire to make the tea and coffee and repeated attempts at striking up conversations about absolutely anything and everything.

Vets

A highly contagious virus that seems to make untalented people feel like they have some sort of duty to put everyone else down all the time.

Woofer

Mainly found in newly promoted managers, making them prone to regular and prolonged bouts of barking at their staff. If not nipped in the bud early enough it can easily turn them into Sergeant Shout.

So, what's your next step?

Polar Bear Pirate Terminology

Albert And Victoria: See viruses
Anteater: See viruses
Arthritic Mountains: A range of man-made mountains found only in the mind
Ask Rackets: Attack or defensive counter-attack questions to put others on the back foot
Badge Boys: See viruses
BC: Before Conditioning
BEDs: Big Exciting Dreams
Belief Thermals: Soaring up and down belief levels
Betamax: See viruses
Betty Backroom: The behind the scenes organizer
Big Boss: The hard disk
Big Chum: See viruses
Big Es: Endorphins
Black Hole BLOATER: A BLOATER responsible for unexplained alien abductions
BLOATERS: Boasting, Lazy, Obnoxious And Tediously Egotistical, Reptilian Saddos
Bobs: See viruses
Boiled Sprout Alarm: A sniff alert that there's a Sinker about
Bubble Wrapping: Popping SMUGs

Bunker Brain: An entrenched mind that is impregnable to new ideas
Card Tarts: See viruses
Cartoon Attitude: The childlike attitude of Polar Bear Pirates
Chewing-Gum Television: TV that is repeated over and over again
Cocoon: A comfy place to stay
Complacency: The cancer of success
Complacency (Town of): Where the Norms live
Corporate Abusers: PUP-nappers who gag talent
Daniel's Derriere: See Viruses
Deck Chairs: Lightweights who allow themselves to be put on
Dignity: Where the Fools are all Kings
DIY Belief: Do It Yourself belief
Dolly: See viruses
Dolly Team: A whole team of clones
DOT Team: A spot-on, focused team benefiting from Diversity Of Thought
Dunk: The art of dipping in and out of the hard disk area to snatch
    good ideas
Egg In Fridge: A real, burning, deep-down need
FAFFing About Time: Family And Friends First time
Fat City: Where the winners live
Fat City Road Map: A map of alternative routes to Fat City
Flash Gone: A smokescreen PBP tactic used to create confusion
Flypaper People: People whose faces attract losers, weirdos and oddballs
44.4: Today's most likely maximum countdown to croak time
Four Bs: The four most likely places to experience a Noddy: Bed, Bog,
    Bath or Bar
The Gap: The small but perilous area between planning and doing
Gob Lobs: See viruses
Graft Grommets: See viruses
Grazer: Someone who snacks out all day
Green Mamba Person: An unnoticed deadly person
Grindstone Cowboy: See viruses
Head Treads: The ladder pullers of Fat City
Heat-Seeking Neg Ferret: An advanced form of Neg Ferret
Hedgehog Heads: Prickly, frightened people whose minds are closed up

Hide And Seek Champions: See viruses
Hissy Pissy Pythons: People working in client-facing roles who
 hate customers
Hitchers: Passengers in teams looking for free rides
Igloo: See viruses
I'm Just: See viruses
Jaffa Gaffa: See viruses
Jellyfish People: Drifting with the flow people
Kak Welders: Those who try to make the best out of nothing
Little Boss: The floppy
London Sparrow: See viruses
Looking Between Your Legs: Seeing things differently
Lucans: See viruses
LUST Relationships: Relationships based on Loyalty, Understanding,
 Sharing and Trust
Maggot Mind: A desire to buzz off out of it
Malcolms: People who are honest about who and what they are
Micro Mind: See viruses
Mind Modem: Modulates and demodulates everything into 3D pictures
Molasses Man: A sweet but slow person burdened by the beliefs
 of others
Neg Ferrets: Seekers of negativity
Neg Fraternity: The brotherhood of Neg Ferrets, Sinkers, BLOATERS and
 Head Treads
Noddies: Brief and creative moments when we slip into our open hard
 disk area
Norms: Average pedestrian people
N'Ts: Negative words used by Sinkers to implant sinking thinking
One Degree Club: A group of extraordinary people who all do that little
 bit extra
Overhead: See viruses
Pants Porters: Those who bring their old team ways with them
PBPs: Polar Bear Pirates
Petal People: Over-sensitive types who drop out quickly
PHPs: Proactively Helpful People

Picture Files: Where people's 3D pictures of their past experiences are saved

Pineapple People: Scary-looking people who are actually very sweet

Pit Stops: Collectable periods of time off work awarded as a team thank-you

Point Plonk: The precise moment beyond which there is no return when dunking

POO: People's Old Opinions

POP: Power Of Picture

Pregnant Problems: Problems ripe with opportunity

Prisoners of POO: Those held back by People's Old Opinions

Pumpkin People: Unnoticed for 364 days of the year until they light up with their annual bright idea

PUPs: Potential-Unhatched Players

PUP-napping: The act of silencing tomorrow's talent

Quitter: Where the Nobodies live

RC'd: Reconditioned

Reagan's: See viruses

Remote Control: A spectator's view of yourself

Rock Bottom: Where most winners come from

Sand Writers: Those who leave their mark behind

SEE Environment: A Solution-Enhanced Environment

Sergeant Shout: A manager who tries to rule by fear

Self Lickers: Those who worship at their own shrine

SELLs: SONAR Effective Leading Leaders

Sinkers: Fat City dropouts trying to sink other people's attempts at reaching it

Sinking Thinking: Negative thinking put into people's heads by Sinkers

SMUGs: Small Unseen Goals

Snapshots: Memorable TNT images of people

Snigger Trigger Tags: Amusing, devious label tags used to quickly locate picture files

Soap Sods: See viruses

SONAR: Sounding Out Needs And Responding

SPAM Heads: Successful People Always Moaning

Spanked: Extremely tired

Spoon Benders: See viruses

Sticky People: People who get bogged down easily

Stop Bombs: No-entry judgements dropped on Fat City travellers by Head Treads

Surf's Up: When everything is just rocking along

Take Away: Exposing an opportunity then taking it away to motivate someone

Time Con: A con used in an attempt to speed up time when doing scummy jobs

Ticking Team: A successful team that's working well

TNTs: Tiny Noticeable Things

TOEs: Tag On Extensions that people add on to their answers

Toilet Team: A team of clones going down the pan

Tonsil Manure: Cultivated bullshit

Truffles In Sewers: Good people who feel very unnoticed

Ugly Butter: Malicious gossip

Velcro Person: See viruses

Venus Punter Trap: A PBP salesperson's closing technique

Venus Rep Trap: A trap set to flush out cold calling sales people

Vets: See viruses

Wet Mondays: Long, miserable faces

Woofer: See viruses

XYs: Unknown people who didn't believe in themselves or life before death

Y-fronts: People who are all front and give it the big Yes but are just pants when it comes to delivering

Zoo Team: A team of talented but restricted people who are forced to behave like animals

The PBP Motto

'si ursus esse vis esto ursus
praedo septentrionalis'